Brighton and Hove

A Second Selection

IN OLD PHOTOGRAPHS

The Peace Statue on the boundary between Brighton and Hove shortly after it was unveiled on 12 October 1912 by the Duke of Norfolk.

Brighton
and Hove

A Second Selection

IN OLD PHOTOGRAPHS

Collected by Judy Middleton

Alan Sutton Publishing Limited
Phoenix Mill · Far Thrupp
Stroud · Gloucestershire

First published 1994

British Library Cataloguing in Publication Data

Middleton, Judy
Brighton and Hove: Second Selection in
Old Photographs. – (Britain in Old
Photographs Series)
I. Title II. Series

ISBN 0-7509-0651-0

Typeset in 9/10 Sabon.
Typsetting and origination by
Alan Sutton Publishing Limited.
Printed in Great Britain by
Redwood Books, Trowbridge.

Contents

Prefects of Hove College in 1941. Left to right: Whapham, Swyer, Craft, Carter, Marshall, with Davies standing in front.

Introduction

This is a book about people. It is interesting to note how sociable people were in days gone by. The majority from young to old belonged to a church, an organization, a club or a society and the high spot of the year was the annual outing. People's horizons were much narrower then and often they did not travel far from the place where they grew up. Therefore a summer outing to Hassocks was an adventure.

Music was important and open air concerts attracted enthusiastic crowds. A top musician like Herr Franz Meisel of the Brighton Corporation Band earned more than the Borough Accountant or the Medical Officer of Health. The numerous churches and chapels were served by large choirs and many people have childhood memories of a Salvation Army Band playing on street corners.

Another aspect of life in those days was the public interest in funerals. The Victorians and Edwardians regarded death as a natural part of life and it was not the taboo subject it has become today. If an important person or someone of local interest died, it was quite natural for the local company to produce a postcard souvenir of the occasion. Perhaps the peak of this fashion was reached in 1910 when King Edward VII died and postcards were sold showing him on his deathbed. We would consider that as outrageous bad taste. Conversely, much of our present way of life would be regarded by them with absolute horror.

This book opens a window into the past and into the lives of ordinary people.

Elizabeth, later Lady Rawson, on her wedding day in 1902. (See caption on page 22.)

SECTION ONE

Transport

The charabanc stands outside Portslade station in around 1927. The vehicle is most probably a Daimler as it looks practically identical to the one on page 18. The difference is that in this photograph the charabanc does not have headlights at the front of the bonnet. Note also the double running board. In the background there are advertisements for 'Captain Blood' and 'The man who Fights Alone'.

A splendid study of the Royal Mail coach in its final days as a horse-drawn service. It was taken in the spring of 1905.

The Royal Mail Parcel Post took its last horse-drawn coach from London to Brighton on 1 June 1905. It is the same driver and assistant as in the previous illustration but not the same horses. The coach was photographed on Clayton Hill – a notorious spot in coaching days when the passengers were sometimes obliged to get out and walk up the hill to spare the horses.

Royal Mail Parcel Post Motor Coach, London to Brighton, at Friars Oak.
The first Journey, June 2nd 1905.

The following day (2 June 1905) the first Royal Mail's Parcel Post by motor coach ran from London to Brighton. Here it is at Friar's Oak with a mechanic bending over it, and some interested spectators looking on. The driver is so well protected from the elements as to be almost invisible; the vehicle's number is LC 552.

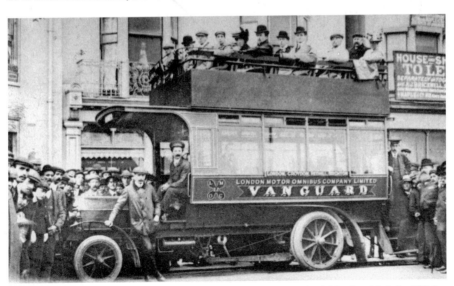

The London-based Vanguard double-decker bus in around 1905. On 12 July 1906 a Vanguard en route to Brighton crashed at Handcross Hill and ten people were killed. Four survivors were rescued by E.A. Eager, Director of the Brighton, Hove and Preston United Omnibus Company who drove a Milnes-Daimler bus to the scene and conveyed the casualties to hospital.

Alfred Tate's Daimler, registration number AP 23. The vehicle took part in the famous Emancipation Run from London to Brighton in 1896. Unfortunately, it also came to grief at Handcross where it overturned. Alfred Tate, who wasn't in the least bit daunted, had it conveyed back to his workshop.

This is the result of Alfred Tate's efforts – the first commercial vehicle in the area, photographed at Portslade in 1908. All he did was to cobble the body and tilt of an ordinary cart onto the chassis. The result was not very sophisticated but then early motoring was a somewhat hit and miss affair. The Tates, for instance, never went motoring without a bag of french nails in case the solid tyres needed to be hammered back on.

Coustick's delivery van in around 1905. Mr W. Coustick senior is seated inside his van with his large delivery basket beside him. He ran a baker's shop at the corner of Trafalgar Road and Victoria Road, Portslade. The photograph was taken by William Wood of Kingston-by-Sea.

The last load, 6 June 1913. It is not a happy occasion; hence the wreath behind the man in the straw boater and the one white and one black horse. This was the last number 10 tram to run between Shoreham and Aldrington. Hove Council was allowed to pull up the tram rails under an Act of Parliament, passed in 1912, in which Hove sought powers to run its own trolley buses. In the end nothing came of it but it was too late for the trams.

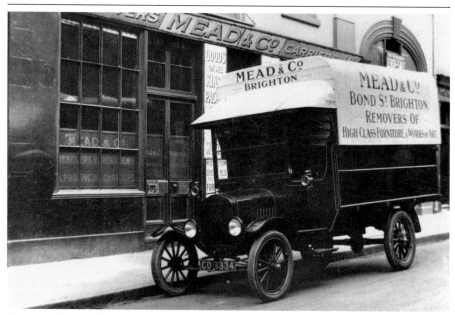

Mead and Co.'s delivery van in around 1912. The business was established at 17 and 18 Bond Street, Brighton in 1912 and the firm also ran auction rooms. By 1966 the firm, still at the same site, had stopped being furniture removers and were only auctioneers.

A portrait of two Morris commercial vehicles belonging to Masters and Smelt and photographed in around 1927. The firm was run from St Nicholas's Road, Portslade, and the vans transported clinker and ash from the power station to the breeze block works run by Mr Tack at the far end of Portslade's goods yard. The registration numbers are PN 5090 and PN 5091.

The charabanc stands outside St Andrew's church hall, Portslade in around 1920. The background is still familiar today but the hall has been demolished and replaced with Tate's car showroom. The vehicle's number is XA 9472. Albert and Olive Pierce stand at the right in front of the charabanc with young Reg Bear.

Children from Middle Street School, Brighton prepare to go on an outing to Arundel in the 1920s. Note the paper streamers. This extraordinary looking vehicle seems to owe a great deal to locomotive design.

This charabanc outing in the 1920s must have enjoyed good weather as all the shops have their blinds drawn down. George and Marie Masters from Portslade occupy the front seat.

A church outing from St Andrew's, Portslade on 22 July 1922. Winifred Drew is seated in the centre wearing a large dark hat and next to her sits Doug Mepham. The happy couple got married in 1925 and, as Doug only earned 25s a week, his father told him he would be better off buying a new pair of boots than getting married. On the left of the coach is the legend 'speed 12 m.p.h.'.

The Ronuk factory outing to Hastings in 1925. Ronuk, maker of the famous red polish, was established at Portslade in 1902 after small beginnings at Providence Place, Brighton. By the time of the photograph Ronuk had already been awarded two royal warrants. On the right stands J. Horace Fowler, founder and managing director, popularly known as 'the Guv'nor'.

Box's Commercial College outing in around 1925. The college was situated at 7 St George's Place, Brighton. The college, whose slogan was 'Be Businesslike', was founded in the 1890s and prided itself on turning out competent stenographers and secretaries. The charabanc is called a Golden Butterfly and the proprietor is Frank Bevan of 7 Queensbury Mews, Brighton.

The Battle of Trafalgar pub in Trafalgar Road, Portslade organized this outing in the 1920s. The vehicle is similar to the ones used in the Ronuk outing but there are differences – for example the double running board does not extend in front of the back wheels.

A Daimler charabanc outing arranged for the staff employed by Albert Pierce of Station Road, Portslade in around 1928. When this photograph was taken Mr Pierce had recently created his double-fronted ironmonger's shop by converting the house where his family used to live next door.

The Dyke Railway station photographed on a summer day in around 1908. The passengers must climb another 200 feet before they can enjoy the extensive views from Devil's Dyke. The Dyke Railway opened in 1887 and a return ticket cost 2s 6d (first class), 1s 8d (second class) and 1s 3d (third class).

Young John Bryon leans over the wooden fence to wave his school cap at the train on the Dyke Railway in around 1934. The last train ran on 31 December 1938.

This view of Hove station will not be immediately recognizable to Hove residents because today the building is obscured by a cast iron and glass canopy. The same footbridge can still be seen to the right however. This is in fact the third station at Hove. The first was a small affair north of Holland Road, erected when the line opened, and the second was situated east of the footbridge.

Brighton Railway station looks somewhat deserted for the mid-morning period. The young woman on the left stands beneath a sign for the 'West Coast Lines', while on the other side of W.H. Smith's bookstall can be seen the notice for the 'East Coast Lines'. Many people will remember the cigar kiosk in the background.

SECTION TWO
Weddings

Rosa May made an exceptionally pretty bride when she married her cousin Frederic Charles Hodder at St Leonard's church, Aldrington in 1901. The bridal photograph was taken in the garden of 33 Carlton Terrace, Portslade, which at that time was a smart address. It is difficult to see details of the bride's high-necked dress, but perhaps it repeats the fashionable tucked sleeves, gathered twice on the upper arm, visible in the bridesmaids' dresses. The bridesmaids are the bride's sisters: Elsie, Mabel, Maud, Lottie and Blanch. Rosa May celebrated her hundredth birthday on 27 May 1976.

A winter wedding in around 1883 when Cecilia de Gamm West married Mr Huxtable. The couple later moved to Hove where Mrs Huxtable kept a lodging house at St Catherine's Terrace. They had four daughters called Gladys, Constance, Katie and Maud. In the photograph note that only one man out of ten is clean shaven. The bride's dress features a tiered skirt and a high neckline.

Elizabeth Robson married Cooper Rawson in 1902. Her dress is a lovely creation with bands of scalloped lace and narrow sleeves which billow out at the wrist. Cooper Rawson served as one of Brighton's two Members of Parliament from 1922 until 1944. He was knighted in 1926. Sir Cooper Rawson gained the distinction of winning his seat with the highest majority ever achieved in a British parliamentary election – the figure was 62,253, in 1931. Lady Rawson became a Justice of the Peace.

On 8 August 1904 Bella Cuttress married John Frost at St Peter's church, Preston. The bride's brother George Cuttress stands on the right – he owned a brewery in Poynings – while on the left is Alderman Burberry. The bride's sisters are the bridesmaids: Louise on the left and Millicent on the right. The bridegroom was a solicitor's clerk and was born in 1855 which made him twenty years older than his bride. They had two children.

Another photograph of the Cuttress-Frost wedding. The two ladies seated at the right are Betty and Mary Blaber who made all the dresses. This involved a great deal of pin tucking and lace edging in the skirts not to mention ruffles at the wrist and draperies on the shoulder. Behind Millicent Cuttress stands George Cuttress and next to him is his wife Amy. Her brother was Henry Cheal, well known for his books on Shoreham.

Gladys Huxtable married William Jenkins, a post office engineer, at All Saints, Hove on 13 July 1913. The photograph was taken at the back of 20 St Catherine's Terrace where the bride's mother kept a lodging house from 1902 until 1916. She is seated at the far left next to the bride's sister Katie. On the far right is Sam Green, proprietor of the nearby Sussex Hotel, and next to him is the bride's grandmother, Mrs West.

This photograph is almost a companion piece to the previous one because it shows the wedding of Glady's sister Katie Huxtable while Gladys herself has graduated to a young matron with baby Cecilia on her knee. It appears that the bride's mother and grandmother wore identical outfits on both occasions, although in the latter Mrs Huxtable has changed her hat while Mrs West has dispensed with one altogether. Katie married Stanley Ashton, an artist, in 1915, also at All Saints.

This wedding dates from about 1917. The bride's dress is short enough to reveal dark buckled shoes and it is in a simple style with a large collar and ruffled inset. Her veil is set low on her forehead and held by a circlet of flowers. The happy couple are Elsie Underhill and Sam Beck. Mr and Mrs David Green, the bride's grandparents, sit next to her. He was an old time Sussex shepherd and he died in 1920 aged ninety-two; his wife followed a week later.

Although the Drews were a Portslade family, Fred Drew married Susan in Suffolk in the 1920s. This was because they were both in service there at a large country house. Fred was butler and Susan was cook. All the dresses have a simple scooped neckline with elbow length sleeves and pin tucks around the hem.

A lovely twenties-style bride poses outside the west door of St Nicolas's church, Portslade in around 1921. She is Cecilia Peters, known as Cissie, and her husband is Len Grigson, one of a brood of thirteen children from Abinger Road. Both are dressed in the height of fashion – note her white two-barred shoes and his splendid Homburg with its wide light band.

The bridal party stand on the steps of All Saints, Hove in 1924 after Lilian Stoneham married Frederick Scrase. The bride's father was James Stoneham who owned a bakery on the corner of Haddington Street and Blatchington Road which he later sold to the Co-op. His son Jim Stoneham played cricket for Sussex. The little bridesmaid, Patricia, later married Norman Wheatley and they emigrated to Australia in the 1960s.

This photograph concentrates on the bridesmaids. It was taken outside the church of the Sacred Heart, Norton Road, Hove in around 1930. Left to right the young ladies are Flora Horner and Louise Horner (cousins) and the girls are Joan Langley (niece of the bridegroom) and Jean Horner (niece of Flora). The dresses are blue with gold thread in the insets and overskirts and the gold is echoed in the flower baskets and shoes of the little girls.

By the 1930s the calf-length wedding dress belonged to the past. This bride has reverted to a traditional long dress with a medieval-style tiara. The photograph was taken in 1936 when Doris Court married Sydney Baker. Mr Baker (known as Pat) later became a Justice of the Peace and was Chairman of Portslade Urban District Council 1958–9.

On 31 July 1937 Gladys Ellis married Vic Banfield. The bride's outfit was blue with pink buttons and she carried a bouquet of pink carnations tied with ribbon. The photograph was taken in the garden of a house in Brasslands Drive, Portslade. In the background stands a mahogany-built railway carriage which was used for storage.

Strangely enough this wedding took place on the same day as the previous one (31 July 1937). The two brides were once pupils together at St Nicolas's School, Portslade but they did not know they shared the same wedding day until they met again by chance in 1990. Kathleen Ford married her first cousin William Ward at Brighton and the bridesmaids are her sisters, Doris on the left and Edith on the right. Edith made the dresses – white satin for the bride and blue material figured with pink for the bridesmaids.

Les Hamilton married Olive King on 3 February 1940 at St Barnabas's church, Hove. On his wedding morning Les received two telegrams – one of congratulations, the other ordering his immediate return to duty. The bridesmaids are Mary King (sister), Joyce Funnell (cousin) and the little girl is Patricia Church. Les later became a councillor and was Chairman of Portslade Urban District Council 1964–5 and Mayor of Hove 1978–9.

A wedding group in May 1941 with a splendid look at wartime fashions. The bride's and bridesmaid's dresses are borrowed. The bridegroom is Harry Reed and his bride is Ivy Jones; they are standing outside Greenways, Portslade. The Reeds were market gardeners.

Another wartime wedding. This took place on 4 April 1942 at St Nicolas's church, Portslade. Reg Forrest wears his RAF uniform while the bride and bridesmaid wear similar but not identical dresses of dusky pink. The bride is Gwendoline Peters and her sister Joan is the bridesmaid.

The bridegroom had recently been demobbed after service with the Royal Signals. William Reed married Joan Biulderbeck on 7 June 1947 at St Nicolas's church, Portslade. The bride's father was a chef.

Florence Reed, the bridesmaid on the right in the last photograph, is herself the bride in this one. She married George Herbert Steele on 16 October 1948 at St Nicolas's church, Portslade. Her wedding outfit was a smart blue two-piece (to which all the family contributed their clothing coupons) with white hat and shoes. Romance blossomed for the couple while serving as members of the Civil Defence at Portslade.

Canadian Joe Taylor from New Brunswick was stationed at Portslade during the Second World War and he used to spend his leave with the Mepham family. His two brothers were killed on active service and Joe himself was a POW for two years and emerged emaciated and ill. He recovered, however, and this is the photograph he sent back to his friends in Portslade to show how he and his bride looked on their wedding day.

This photograph was taken in July 1947 outside the Methodist church in Portland Road, Hove. The bride Rosemary Brown carried a bouquet of red roses and she wore a pearl tiara. Her bridesmaids were dressed in pink floral tafetta and carried pink roses. The bridegroom is Gurth Hughes, a chartered accountant. Nobody knows the identity of the interested granny on the right.

Bob Gill and his bride Gwen (Mills) came out of St Nicolas's church, Portslade on 21 June 1952 to be greeted by a scout guard of honour. Bob and Gwen took a keen interest in scouting and in 1976 Bob was awarded the Silver Acorn to be followed by the Silver Wolf in 1985.

SECTION THREE

Fire!

The Brighton Volunteer Fire Brigade at 4 Duke Street in around 1905. The black dog in the foreground wears a magnificent collar engraved with the words 'Stop me not, but onward let me jog, for I am Bob the Brighton firemen's dog. To Bob, for British pluck, from Miss Ada Chappell'. Bob was a stray who lived at the fire station for twelve years, attending fires with the men and always first to be ready at turnouts. He helped with the hose cart by hanging on to the cord attached to it all the way to the fire. But Bob knew the difference between a real alarm and a practice and when the latter took place nothing could make him stir, no matter how violently the bell rang. Bob died on 10 September 1907.

Brighton's new motor tender in around 1907 designed by Superintendent Lacroix. He had overall control of both the Police Fire Brigade and the Volunteer Fire Brigade. In the photograph the back doors are open to reveal the closely packed hose which was 600 feet long. The tender also carried a ladder, a variety of tools, hydrant fittings and a jumping sheet.

Two members of the Hove Fire Brigade in around 1908. Cadet Edward Brown is on the left and his father Frederick Brown stands on the right. Mr Brown ran a builder's business at the top of Westbourne Street. The premises were fitted with a bell and a private wire to the Fire Station. When the bell rang, Mr Brown would hurriedly down tools, pull on his uniform and take the hand cart to the scene. Although the fire engine was housed in George Street, various items of fire fighting equipment were kept in depots dotted around Hove, including Westbourne Street.

A splendid portrait of an old fire engine. It appears to be a double vertical model produced by Shand, Mason and Co. It dates from the 1890s and was the standard type of horse-drawn engine. The Gas Works maintained its own fire brigade.

Victor Lacroix was the Brighton Fire Superintendent from 1888 until 1921. His headquarters were at Preston Circus (established 1901) where this photograph was taken. On 1 January 1901 Superintendent Lacroix had a narrow escape when fire broke out at Jay's Furnishing Stores, 127 Queen's Road, Brighton. He was inside the building directing operations but had to be rescued by colleagues who lowered a life-line to him and so saved him from falling through the charred floor timbers to the basement. Two floors were burned through.

The Portslade Gas Works Fire Brigade in the 1920s. Herbert Mepham is seated third from the left, front row; he also drove the Gas Works ambulance. Doug Mepham is standing second from right, back row. The men proudly exhibit their recently won trophy. There was bad feeling in Portslade in 1906 when two men who apparently belonged to both brigades opted to compete with the Gas Works' side in the National Fire Brigade competition, thus weakening the Portslade team. After that Portslade Council made it a rule that their firefighters could not belong to any other brigade.

The Portslade Fire Brigade in around 1912. The collecting box is for the Hospital Fund. The two men on the right are wearing the long service medals of the National Fire Brigades Union to which they were entitled after ten years' service. The brigade was formed in 1900 after detailed consultations with Fire Superintendent Lacroix. The Fire Station was erected in 1909.

Portslade Fire Brigade together with some of the Gas Works Brigade one of whom is Alfred Eastwood, third from the right. The man with the flat cap seated in the centre is the stopcock whose duty it was to turn off the mains in one street to increase water pressure in the next. On 28 June 1905 Portslade Fire Brigade won fifth place in open competition with the whole of England and Wales at the Crystal Palace.

A fête held in the grounds of Windlesham House School would not be complete without the attendance of Portslade Fire Brigade. George Pierce is standing in the back row, third from left, and Captain A.W. Hillman stands in the front. He was appointed in 1903.

Perhaps the caption should be 'still competing'. This is the Gas Works Fire Brigade in 1937 when their prizes included the Motor Wet and the Motor Turnout and Escape. One fifth of the men shown here belonged to the same family. Herbert Mepham is behind the wheel, Doug Mepham stands behind the left-hand shield and Stan Mepham stands on the far left at the rear of the ladder.

The mayor and mayoress of Hove inspect the new motor fire engine outside the Town Hall, 23 September 1920. It was purchased from Dennis Brothers Ltd of Guildford for £1,360. The vehicle accommodated 1,500 feet of hose, an escape ladder, a hydraulic hose reel and a forty gallon tank. In addition it could seat four men on either side with the driver and officer in front. Horses were no longer necessary and the old steam fire engine was disposed of for £125.

The aftermath of a fire at St Peter's church, Preston, 23 June 1906. The fire originated in the organ loft and badly damaged the ancient frescoes. Fortunately the flames did not reach the chancel, and the register, dating back to 1555, was undamaged in its iron box. Twenty-five firemen attended the scene and the water pressure from their hoses was so strong that roof tiles were scattered in all directions.

This photograph is one of a series taken of the destruction of Mr Lewonski's furniture depository at 4 Shirley Street, Hove, on 18 April 1908. When the alarm was raised several men were still inside and three horses were stabled nearby; all were rescued. The flames were so fierce that Hove's four hoses had little effect and the Brighton contingent were sent for. Soon Superintendent Lacroix and his men came tearing up on their motor fire engine closely followed by the Volunteer Fire Brigade from Duke Street. Their efforts were somewhat hampered by hordes of onlookers.

The Priory at Withdean, built in 1882, was badly damaged by fire in June 1910. The weather had been hot and sultry and, when the storm finally broke, there was continuous sheet lightning which struck both chimneys and the house caught fire. Debris fell from the roof, smashing the glass roof of the conservatory and badly denting the helmets worn by Superintendent Lacroix and Fireman Milner.

There was a fire at the Hove Lawns Hotel in December 1910. It gutted the building from floor to ceiling leaving only the billiard room at the back unscathed. The fire appeared to have started before 4 a.m. in the smoking room. Mrs Mayhead, wife of the proprietor, raised the alarm and both Mayheads, their three children, the cook and the barman struggled through the smoke to the balcony over the entrance. There they were let down to the street by means of the hanging lamp and with the assistance of PC Aldridge.

SECTION FOUR
Children

A charming study of Andrew Melville and his son John in around 1934. Mr Melville was the proprietor of the Grand Theatre, North Road, Brighton. Tragically he died on 4 March 1938 when John was still only seven years old. During the war John was evacuated aboard the *Orduna* to Nassau in the Bahamas where the Duke and Duchess of Windsor took an interest in the evacuees and gave them parties.

Edith Annie Ford photographed in around 1900 by W. Wright of 26 George Street, Hove. Her parents lived in Cowper Street where the baby was born. Some unknown benefactor left a basket of beautiful baby clothes on the doorstep for the new arrival and Mrs Ford was so delighted she took the baby to be photographed wearing them.

Hector Coustick and his sister in around 1902. Their father kept the bakery and post office on the corner of Victoria Road and Trafalgar Road, Portslade. Hector's wide-brimmed straw hat was a fashionable item for children at that time.

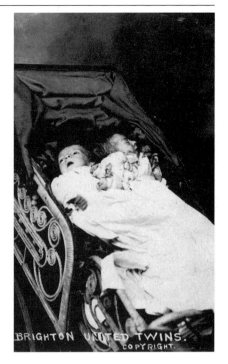

The Brighton united twins were Daisy and Violet Hilton who were born on 5 February 1908 at Harrington Road, Brighton. They were delivered by Dr James Augustus Rooth and adopted by a midwife. The Hiltons are the only known British siamese twins to survive to maturity. The girls became talented stage artists and appeared at the Brighton Hippodrome. They could sing, play the piano, the saxophone and clarinet as well as dance and perform a comic routine. They died on 5 January 1969.

These two smartly dressed girls were photographed in Portslade in around 1908. They are Cissie Peters (left) and Dorothy Oden. Dorothy's parents ran a bakery at 95 Abinger Road. Cissie's brother Fred served in the East Surrey Regiment during the First World War and was killed on 1 November 1918 just ten days before the armistice.

Gwendoline Peters with the huge bow and the long ringlets was aged three when this study was taken in 1919. Her father Frank Peters was the maintenance foreman at Portslade Gas Works. He was also the goalkeeper for the Gas Works' football team. When Gwendoline grew up she married Reg Forrest, pictured below in his schooldays.

The photographer from Eastbrook Road, Portslade obviously hoped to drum up some business by making school photographs into seasonal greetings cards. This was taken in 1922 when Reg Forrest was a pupil at St Andrew's School, Portslade.

Norman Daniel Shaw wearing his sailor suit in 1911. The name Daniel was something of a tradition in the family and four generations of Shaws, all with Daniel as one of their Christian names, were involved in the running of Shaw's Stores in Hove. The store was founded in 1862 by Norman's grandfather Daniel Shaw. Norman Shaw retired in 1964 and the store closed down.

Two choir boys from St Patrick's church, Cambridge Road, Hove, in 1927. On the left is Charles Leonard Caperon (born 10 January 1915) and his brother George William Caperon (born 4 May 1918) is on the right. At the time there were twelve men and boys in the choir. This was something of a come down from the church's glory days when St Patrick's was renowned for its music and could boast a choir of eighty surpliced men and boys. Critics dubbed it 'Paddy's Music Hall'.

A delightful study of juvenile fashions captured on a school treat at Portslade in 1914. The little girl in the centre wears a lacy bonnet reminiscent of the one worn by little Miss Coustick on page 42 while the girl third from right is up to date in her dress with dropped waist and handkerchief-point style hem. Sailor suits for boys are still popular.

Bill Ring at his grandparents' house in Old Shoreham Road, Portslade in around 1944. The family story goes that Bill spotted the teddy bear in a shop window and refused to budge until his parents went in to purchase it. Note the little coat with the velvet collar – a style made popular by the royal children.

Streets and Houses

74 BRIGHTON. — The Market early morning. — LL.

A busy market scene outside Brighton Town Hall early one morning in around 1908. People in the surrounding countryside who had produce to sell used to hitch up the horse and cart while it was still dark, hang a paraffin lamp on either side and set off for market. By 6 a.m. the produce would be laid out ready to sell. The horses were stabled nearby until needed and at some stage the men would make for a tea shop in Bartholomews which sold steaming mugs of tea and doorstep sized sandwiches.

West Street in around 1907. On the left is the rebuilt Olde King's Head where Charles II met Captain Nicholas Tettersell who later safely conveyed him to France aboard the coal brig *Surprise*. In memory of the king, the inn used to hang up an oak tree branch every Oak-apple Day (29 May) until 1830. This building was demolished in 1933.

A later view of West Street taken in around 1912. On the right is the Half Moon pub and further up is the Academy cinema opened on 6 June 1911. There were Moorish-style arches dating from the time the building was constructed as a Turkish Baths in 1868. The Academy became so popular that it was remodelled in 1913. Unfortunately the Moorish arches went in the 1930s and the whole building was demolished in 1974.

A view of Queen's Road and the Clock Tower in around 1912. On the left are the premises of the Royal Exchange Assurance Co. and next door is T. Lulham and Son, boot manufacturer. The arched porch and hanging lamp belong to the Royal Hotel and further on there is the White Lion Hotel. Opposite is the Quadrant Hotel run by Mrs Bovey.

A view of Queen's Road in around 1925. On the left is the Liverpool Globe Insurance Co. at 32A and Gadd's Hotel run by James Finneran is at No. 35. On the right the Pickford's sign is visible at roof level.

The Hippodrome in around 1923. In 1897 there was a 'Real Ice Skating Palace' at 53–58 Middle Street. Later this was converted to the Hippodrome from the designs of Frank Matcham who was also the architect of the London Hippodrome. In 1902 the Brighton Hippodrome was called 'one of the handsomest Palaces of Amusement in the Kingdom'.

Grand Parade in around 1905 demonstrating what a pleasant place it was for a quiet promenade. The houses were occupied by a mixture of professional and private residents and some were boarding houses.

A view looking north towards Pavilion Buildings in around 1910. The corner property on the left has not yet been absorbed into Hannington's. In mid-Victorian times Treacher's Library was noted for the politeness of its librarian. On the right, near the clock, is the Pavilion Creamery run by G. Morley.

At first glance it looks as though there is a medieval structure in Lewes Road, Brighton similar to the Barbican at Lewes. In fact it is a piece of Victorian Gothic and marks the entrance to Brighton Extra Mural Cemetery. At the time this scene was recorded in around 1909 the gateway led to a beautiful avenue lined with elm and ilex trees.

Roneo's shop in King's Road, Brighton in around 1915. Roneo's sold office appliances. It was situated at No. 26, between Harrison's Family Hotel on the right, and the Hollywood and Brighton Court Hotel on the left.

The elegant sweep of Adelaide Crescent, Hove, photographed in 1906 with the only traffic being a lone cyclist. Note the railings on the left which enclosed the private gardens. The postcard, sent by someone who worked in one of the houses on the opposite side of the street, says 'I like my place very much I am out on the carriage every day now'. The card was sent to Maud who used to work at the house marked with an X.

Looking north along Westbourne Street, Hove in around 1923. The chimney is part of the generating station belonging to the Hove Electric Lighting Company near Leighton Road. On the left the corner shop at 73 Portland Road is H. Greenfield's, pork butcher, and on the right is E. Foulser, grocer and tea and coffee merchant at 71 Portland Road.

A snow scene at Hove Park Villas on Sunday 26 March 1911. The weather was certainly changeable that year as only the previous Wednesday the temperature had been 61 degrees. There was a further snow storm on 5 April 1911 when six inches fell. The bad weather was good news for the unemployed as 360 of them were hired to clear the streets. The shops on the left are Warren and Son, greengrocers; Francis Smith, wine and spirit merchant; and Day and Hill, fruiterers.

A summer view of Waterloo Street in around 1916. On the left is the historic Hove Lawns Hotel which had been open for business since at least 1828. Note the advertisement for the Imperial Garage, Brunswick Street East.

Looking west towards St John's church *c.* 1908. The church was consecrated on 24 June 1854 and the tower and spire were added in around 1870. On the right are the luxurious Palmeira Mansions erected in 1884 with its private roadway and wall. This wall has recently been restored to its former glory, winning several awards for Hove Council.

A beautifully clear view of the late lamented Hove Town Hall, destroyed by fire in 1966. The imposing tower held a carillon of twelve bells and there were two barrels each containing seven tunes. On Saturday it was a choice of 'God Save the King' or 'Rule Britannia'.

The sea-front road at Hove in 1904 before it was called the Kingsway. The light coloured building on the left is now known as the Sackville Hotel but it was built in 1904 as four separate houses selling at £7,000 each. It became a hotel in 1926.

Although this view looking east down the High Street, Portslade was only taken in May 1963, the foreground has altered considerably. On the left are the two Swiss Cottages and on the right an old pair of cottages which stood on the corner of Windlesham Close. All of them were demolished in the 1960s to make the road less of a blind spot.

The famous and much photographed bridge over the High Street, Portslade. The bridge spanned the two parts of the estate which belonged to Portslade House, a Georgian mansion whose grounds stretched south to the Old Shoreham Road. The bridge was demolished in 1946 to enable double-decker buses to travel up the hill.

High Street, Portslade, looking west in around 1905. The two boys on the left are standing on the steps leading to Hangleton Court, a group of about twelve small flint cottages. Later the land was sold to the owner of Whychcote and the cottages were demolished. In their place a tennis court and greenhouse were built.

An apparently deserted Portslade village c. 1938. On the left the new houses are built on the site of the Grange, demolished in around 1927. They are set further back from the road. On the right stands the George Inn, which was completely rebuilt in around 1933. The pub was not renamed the St George until 1958. In the background are the Swiss Cottages.

Church Road Portslade in 1909. The children are waiting for the Hospital Sunday church parade to begin. Note the scaffolding on the left surrounding the newly built fire station. On the right is the capacious St Andrew's Vicarage. Missing from the photograph is the Catholic church which was not built until 1912.

Boundary Road and Station Road in around 1910. These children are standing virtually on the boundary between Hove and Portslade. Originally, both portions were called Station Road but Hove decided to rename its side Boundary Road in 1903, to avoid confusing people who expected Hove railway station to be at the top of the road.

The Old Shoreham Road, Portslade in around 1908. This view has been completely changed because of road widening schemes in the 1970s. Everything in the photograph has been demolished except the houses in the far distance. The advertisement for Rock Ales is painted on the side of the Southern Cross pub.

Looking east along the Old Shoreham Road in around 1908. The shop is situated on the corner of Wolseley Road. There are advertisements for Cadbury's Cocoa, Fry's chocolate, Nestle's milk, Lyons tea and 'Clark's Bread. Most Easily Digested'. The houses were all swept away in the 1970s.

A meet of the Brighton Brookside Harriers at Patcham Place, 16 December 1914. The Harriers wore dark green coats and were founded by John Brooker Vallance. They met three times a week in the season to chase hares all over the Downs. At the time of the photograph Patcham Place was still in private hands; it was not purchased by Brighton Corporation until 1926.

The Southdown Foxhounds meet at North House Farm, Portslade in 1924. The Huntsman, Joe Mackarness (Mack) is seen mounted on the left. North House Farm was a mixed farm covering a large area. There were cattle and sheep, fields of barley, oats and wheat and down in the valley market gardening including many gooseberry and blackcurrant bushes and greenhouses for the tomatoes.

Grasshopper Cottage in St Ann's Well Gardens, Hove in around 1908. The cottage was so called because it stood in the Grasshopper's Tennis Ground and provided a changing room for members. The cottage and the tennis courts predate the time when Hove Corporation purchased the grounds for a public park in 1906.

This house photographed in around 1908 was called Hillbrow. It stood on 7 acres of land on the west side of Mile Oak Road and was owned by Marianne Stallabrass. Rowan Close now covers the site.

Portslade Farm in around 1908. This too was once owned by Marianne Stallabrass and comprised 87 acres of land with grazing for about two hundred sheep. In the background are farm buildings which were later demolished when Windlesham Close was laid out in the 1930s.

Hove Seaside Villas in around 1912. Plans for the first three houses at the east end were dated 19 January 1909 and reveal that the villas boasted twelve inch concrete walls. They were built for Mr P. Baxter of Glendor Road.

A charming summer study of the pleasures of getting away from it all, taken in around 1928; in this case a holiday home on the Downs Estate at Woodingdean which was quite rural then. The photograph depicts Clovis Warren and her friends. In the background the Downs Hotel can be seen.

Arthur Gates outside 17 Carlton Terrace, Portslade in 1907. Carlton Terrace was an area of better housing but it suffered from being somewhat isolated. For example in 1903 the residents sent a petition to the council protesting about the 'offensive smells arising from refuse and offal deposited in the course of husbandry on land situated on the north side of Portslade Station'.

William Philp and his family outside their home at 26 South Street, Portslade in around 1906. The house is still there, next to the newsagents.

Ethel Chandler and her sister Hilda in front of their house at 79 Trafalgar Road, Easter 1923. These houses were spacious for Portslade, having accommodation on four floors.

Industry

This photograph of Portslade Gas Works was taken on 23 November 1964, looking west. A new petrol plant is being built. Note the chimneys: the two new ones in the foreground belong to A Station; then come two old ones also belonging to A Station and in the background are two at either end of the Electricity Works. The Gas Works started off in a small way in 1870 on 7 acres of land, but by 1926 the works covered 40 acres.

The interior of Portslade Gas Works in the 1930s, looking efficient and clean. In the bad old days, around the time of the First World War, working conditions for the men were terrible. Town gas was more noxious than North Sea gas and sometimes a worker would be overcome by fumes. He was taken out into the fresh air and given milk to drink to absorb the poison. If he went home sick he lost pay. The stink of the greeny-red oxide clung to the skin and clothes of the men and much of south Portslade as well.

The Gas Works 12th Annual Sports, 1 September 1923. The sports field was situated south of the canal and in the background can be seen the main Gas Works building. The one advantage of employment at the Gas Works was the strong community spirit. They ran their own football and cricket teams too.

Saunders and Son in around 1910. This building firm was established in 1889 at 165–7 Edward Street, Brighton. Saunders continued trading in Edward Street until around 1950.

These workers photographed in around 1910 were most probably employed at the Wish Brickfield which was situated between New Church Road and Portland Road, Hove. In 1911 a petition was sent to Hove Council asking that the Wish Brickfield should be 'speedily closed' under the Town Planning Act. Brickmaking had been taking place on the same site since the 1890s and before Aldrington was annexed to Hove.

In the centre foreground Holland Road bisects Cromwell and Davigdor Roads. The scene dates from about 1910. The chimney belongs to the electricity generating station established in the 1890s.

This photograph was taken in 1902 and shows the second electricity generating station to be built at Hove. The chimney was erected by W.A. Field and Co. The site was north of the railway line and St Joseph's Home can be seen in the distance. In 1914 Hove Council purchased the Hove Electric Light Company and ran it until 1947. They were extremely sorry when nationalization came, as providing electricity for their inhabitants had proved their most profitable enterprise.

The Brewery, Portslade, in around 1910. The brewery was founded in 1849 by John Dudney. He rebuilt it in 1881 and it remained the same as it appears here until the 1920s when, under new management, the attractive roof was removed and a new top storey added.

Portslade Brewery workers in around 1920. The brewery was famous for its Southdown Ales made from water drawn from its own deep well. By the 1890s 10,000 gallons an hour were being pumped up to the reservoir at the top of the building. The brewery had its own stables and shoeing forge and its own coopers to make the barrels.

One of the packing rooms at Ronuk's factory at Portslade in around 1926. Mr Fowler, owner and founder of the firm, was an enlightened employer who provided many benefits for his staff. There was a welfare supervisor and matron, a thrift club and a savings club, a sports ground of 7 acres where tennis and stoolball were played, and also a bowling green.

This view dates from about 1910. The road leads up from John Eede Butt's timber yard and in front of the jetty belonging to the Britannia wharf can be seen a timber pond. Wood seasoned in this way was easier to steam into curved timbers. At least this was a tidier way of storing timber than in the old days when timber was dumped anywhere in the water. The harbour commissioners had to regulate the situation and by 1854 timber ponds were only allowed on the north side of the canal.

Portraits

Sergeant Jesse Burchell, photographed in around 1880, was Hove's first police sergeant. In 1874 the twenty-four policemen employed by the old Hove Police Commissioners were reappointed by the newly constituted Hove Commissioners. Among their number was Sergeant Burchell, who earned £1 15s 6d a week. In the photograph he holds the helmet issued for the first time in 1879, costing 12s 6d each. It carries the old Hove badge consisting of a St Andrew's cross and three martlets.

A rare reminder of a family which was once prominent in the area. Alfred Scrase was pictured in 1864 by Wells and Grey. His forbears were established at West Blatchington by 1490, at Hove in the 1630s and at Brighton by the 1770s.

Mercy Scrase, wife of Alfred, was obviously not a lady to be trifled with – perhaps she did not enjoy having to sit still so long for her portrait, taken in 1864. Her maiden name was Daynes-Wood and she and Alfred had five children.

Mr and Mrs J. Durtnall, photographed in 1864 in the studio of Wells and Grey, 144 Western Road, Brighton. He had a well-known business at 149 North Street, Brighton, where he presided over a large warehouse. Durtnall's were also railway and general carriers. The business was well established by 1848 and lasted until 1928.

This portrait of Daniel Shaw was taken in around 1890 by Burt Sharp of 79 West Street, Brighton. Mr Sharp carried an advertisement on the reverse of the photograph proclaiming 'Studio for Artistic Photography. Patronized by Her Most Gracious Majesty the Queen'. Daniel Shaw was the founder of Shaw's Stores which stood on the north side of Church Road adjacent to George Street.

Robert Horne Penney and his grandson A.G.W. Penney in 1900. Mr Penney came from Poole originally but settled at Southwick where he became the largest ship owner in the area. He was also one of the Shoreham Harbour Trustees. As a Quaker he would not allow any liquor aboard his ships which may have had something to do with his good record as regards loss of life in shipwrecks. He opened a head office at Brighton in 1879.

The Drew family dressed in their best and looking rather solemn in around 1906. Left to right they are Fred Drew, Philip and Mary, with Winifred and Frederick in front. The boys were twins and the family lived in Wellington Road, Portslade. Fred Drew came from Totnes to look for work in Portslade. He was a carter then but, by the time his daughter Winifred married, on Boxing Day 1925, he was employed as a labourer. Winifred worked as a domestic and her husband and father-in-law were fitters at the Gas Works.

John Turner joined Hove Police in 1890. This photograph was taken in 1907 with a life-belt prominently displayed as he seems to have made something of a career in rescuing people from drowning. He saved two men on 25 May 1905 and two ladies on 18 September 1905. On 16 August 1906 a soldier was bathing his horse when he was swept into the sea and PC Turner rescued him. He saved two more people in September 1907. Each time Hove Council awarded him a guinea for his 'meritorious conduct'.

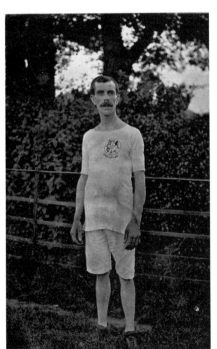

This man with the extraordinary physique was in fact the holder of two Olympic gold medals in 1908. George Larner was a Brighton policeman who had retired from competitive walking but the chief constable allowed him time off from police duties to continue training. The chief constable's faith was amply rewarded when Larner carried off the gold for the 3,500 metre walk and the gold for the 10 mile walk.

Alfred Vanderbilt was a handsome American millionaire with a passion for coaching. The Venture was his first coach and it arrived outside the Metropole on 8 May 1908 to a rapturous welcome from the public. In this photograph guard Walter Godden stands on the left and Vanderbilt is on the right. Vanderbilt also owned the Old Times, both coaches being painted in the Vanderbilt colours of maroon and white with red lines. Tragically, Vanderbilt drowned on 7 May 1915 when the *Lusitania* went down, having given his life-belt to a young nurse. He could not swim.

Dr Leonard Hedley Burrows was vicar of Hove and suffragen bishop of Lewes from 1909 until 1914. He was undoubtedly the most photographed cleric in Sussex, captured at football matches, cricket matches, fêtes and open-air meetings. Note the old-fashioned clerical gear – the voluminous lawn sleeves gathered at the wrist in a pie-crust frill, the wide stole and the odd square hat reminiscent of Archbishop Cranmer.

Arthur Gates taught at St Nicolas's School, Portslade from 1908 until he joined the Territorials in 1914. Another Portslade resident, a Mr Still, had the shock of his life somewhere near the front line in France when a dispatch rider came to a halt and it turned out to be Arthur Gates. The war took its toll and Gates died in 1925 leaving his widow to bring up two children on her own.

This portrait was taken during the First World War. On the left is William Denyer, son of George Denyer of the well-known undertaking firm, and on the right is Charles Stoneham. Happily both survived the war. William Denyer later became manager of H.J. Paris, the Hove builders; Charles Stoneham took up tailoring and ran his own business at Upper North Road, Brighton.

Arthur Daniel Shaw was photographed in 1917 wearing his chain of office as President of the Brighton, Hove and District Grocers' and Provision Merchants' Association.

This splendid study shows Ellen Denyer, daughter of George Denyer, dressed for serious war work in 1914. The same style of dress was worn by all the girls who worked on munitions at the Allen West factory, Lewes Road, Brighton.

Marie Mitchell (later Mrs Masters) wearing the uniform of a Southdown bus conductoress in around 1917. Family legend relates that she considered the skirt to be too long and shortened it herself.

This charming portrait of Daisy Pratt was taken in the 1920s. She was a member of the Portslade Salvation Army which was established on 2 August 1882. The Portslade Corps was the 296th in the first three hundred.

Andrew Melville with his poster and pot of glue during his electioneering campaign. He unsuccessfully contested the St Nicholas Ward in Brighton in 1926, 1927 and 1929 but he later served for many years on Portslade Council. He was an actor as well as being the proprietor of the Grand Theatre, North Road, Brighton. One of his best known roles was as Sweeny Todd, the demon barber. His catchphrase 'I'll polish 'em off' used to be shouted out by youngsters up in the gods.

John Broomfield pictured in 1936 with the cups he won at three separate agricultural shows for 'Best Butcher's Beast'. In his heyday he farmed well over 300 acres at Portslade, comprising North House Farm, Stonery Farm and Mile Oak Farm (all of which he owned) and Easthill Farm which he rented from Brighton Corporation.

Interiors

The entrance hall at Whychcote, Portslade, in 1938. It was a house built in the Victorian grand manner with nine bedrooms, two bathrooms and two reception rooms. Even the hall measured 25 feet by 10 feet 6 inches. Oak was used for the floors, panelling, beams and cornices. There was also a large garden. Andrew Melville lived here for ten years and after he died in 1938 Whychcote was sold for £10,000.

The central hall of Brighton Aquarium in 1904. The columns are of granite and marble with some interesting marine details in the capitals. The Aquarium was opened to the public in 1872 and purchased by Brighton Corporation in 1901.

The Victoria Lending Library, Brighton in around 1905. It was so named because Queen Victoria celebrated her Golden Jubilee in 1889 and the library was opened on 16 October of the same year. It housed a stock of 17,545 volumes.

The Winter Garden at the Hotel Metropole in around 1905. Tea dances were held here and at one time there was a large cage full of budgerigars too. The Winter Garden was destroyed in 1960 when the hotel was extended.

The Convalescent Police Seaside Home was built in 1893 at Portland Road, Hove. The sitting room was photographed in 1909. Note the huge case of stuffed birds, the gramophone complete with large horn by the window and the small organ on the right. The home was the first of its kind in the country and received many donations.

The Pavilion Creamery at 6 and 7 Pavilion Buildings, Brighton in around 1910 when George Morley was running it. The décor had a curious mixture of Chinese and Indian motifs, just like the Royal Pavilion itself. The notice on the left states that coffee and cigarettes are served in the Smoking Room.

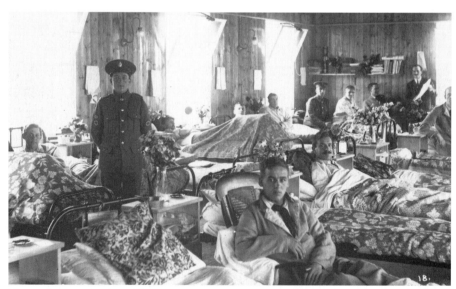

The 2nd Eastern General Hospital, Portland Road, Hove in 1915. The hospital was housed in the Portland Road schools but these soldiers are in a temporary hut. Because the hospital was there Lt-Col. A.J. Rooth made an urgent plea and the cost of making good the appallingly rough surface of School Road was shared between the Duke of Portland and Hove Council.

Rolt's Gymnasium, Holland Road in about 1915. It was known originally as Moss' Gymnasium and was erected in 1883. Later it was owned by Percy S. Rolt who sold it in 1928. It was then converted into a synagogue which was consecrated in 1930.

The Clarence Hotel, North Street, Brighton in around 1930. The hotel was built in 1785 and called the New Inn. The *Lewes Journal* stated 'a coffee house and tavern has just been opened in North Street – a thing never before attempted in Brighton'.

This is the entrance foyer of the Pavilion Cinema, North Street, Portslade in 1936. A presentation of a certificate from the Humane Society is being made to twelve year old Frank Lucas by Councillor Harry Parker. Frank and the council workmen on either side of him, Philip McCarthy and Albert J. Stevens, had all attempted to rescue a boy from drowning in a deep pool near St Andrew's Road.

The Georgian Room at Hove Museum was opened on 18 September 1948. All the pieces on display were created between 1710 and 1790, the idea being to show visitors how a room of that period might have been furnished. The room included examples of Hepplewhite and Chippendale furniture, with an Adam chimney piece.

SECTION NINE

Sport

A cricket match at a fête in around 1898. Note the marquee in the background and the two music stands. Fred Streeter holds a bat in the second row from the front. The photograph was taken by R. Armitage of 112 Portland Road, Hove.

Old Folks' Cricket Match, Portslade, 1929. The combined ages of the men involved is 1,550 years! None of the front row have been identified. In the second row, second from left, is Harry Wakeham (labourer at Broomfield's Farm), fourth from left is Charlie Ayres (roadsweeper), sixth from left is Tom Steel (undertaker), seventh from left is Fred Steele (greengrocer) and eighth from left is Billy Kerr (chimney sweep). In the third row Mr Chatfield is in a bowler and white jacket and next to him stands Mr Broomfield (farmer) wearing a flat cap.

The Sussex County Cricket Ground at Hove in 1908. Present-day spectators may find the view a little difficult to recognize because of the chimney stack and the large group of buildings on the right. The chimney belongs to the electricity generating station in Davigdor Road and to the right are the Davigdor Schools.

Sussex v. Worcester, Hove, 1910. The match took place on 29, 30 and 31 August and was largely ruined by rain. It ended in a draw, but the high spots included Robert Relf (Sussex) giving a superb display of batting by scoring one hundred in just over two hours.

The Sussex v. Surrey match took place on 24, 25 and 26 August 1911. It was not a particularly happy time for Sussex who had no chance of winning with their poor batting. The best batting to be seen was from the Surrey players, J.C. Hobbs and M.C. Bird.

Another view of the Sussex v. Surrey match of 1911. A comfortable way to watch was with the tea tent near at hand. The man in the top hat is the Bishop of Lewes.

Sussex v. Warwick, Hove, 1913. The match was played on 25, 26 and 27 August and Sussex won by six wickets. In the opinion of the experts Warwick would have been defeated more easily had Albert Relf been put on to bowl earlier. He took five wickets.

The Gas Works Cricket Team on 26 June in around 1936. In the back row, third from left, is Alf Eastwood, fourth from right is Albert Mepham and on the far right stands Frank Peters. In the front row, third from right, is Arthur Candy and second from the right is William Peters. In the background are the buildings belonging to Cottesmore, a private boys' school.

A group of Sussex badminton players standing outside the Sussex County Sports Club at Hove in the 1920s. Left to right: Mary Arno, Cathy Evans, -?-, Muriel Anderson, 'Baby' Riley, -?-, Nigel Sharp, Mr Lawrence, Mr Friend-James, -?-, Colonel Riley.

St Andrew's School football team, 1923–4 season, Portslade. In the back row on the far right is John Miles, headmaster, and next to him is Arthur Henry Gates who taught at St Nicolas's School before the war.

St Nicolas's School football team, Portslade in 1932. Back row, left to right: Ray Broadbank, Joe Figgins, John Whiting, J.W. Burn (headmaster). Second row: Johnnie Meaking, Squib Nelson, Johnnie French. Third row: Bill Peters, Les Hamilton (now Councillor L.E. Hamilton), Cyril Peters, Jackie Powell, Herbert Darling. Front row: Harold Reynolds, Horace Hamper and Purdy.

Brighton and Hove Albion Football Club reserves in 1921. In January 1922 Cook, who played for the reserves, nearly had his moment of glory. Albion was in a terrible state: Groves was in bed with a chill, Doran was unfit with an ankle injury, Thompson had a strained thigh and Feebury was barely recovered from flu. The team was announced half an hour before kick-off and Cook was chosen. Unfortunately, however, he lived at Cuckfield and nobody had warned him to be at the ground. In the event Albion beat 1st Division Sheffield United by one goal to nil.

The second round of the Southern Charity Cup on 19 October 1910 at the Goldstone. A thousand spectators saw Albion win by two goals to Reading's nil. The spectators are in the southern stand which was used from 1904 until 1954. The stand came from Preston Park where it had been used in an agricultural show.

The Sussex Wednesday Cup semi-final in around 1910 between Hove Traders and Portland Wednesday. The reason it was called the Wednesday Cup was that Wednesday was the only half day that most shop workers received.

The Brighton reserves in around 1910. Back row, far right: Emmett; front row: Vaughan, Broadfoot and Seymour. They look like ordinary hockey players but if you look at the feet you will see that they are wearing roller skates. The photograph was taken by R. Stewart of 3 Ship Street.

Shops and Pubs

Hanningtons' annual outing in 1920. It is interesting to see a full complement of men on the staff after the manpower drain of the war years. Hanningtons catered for all sorts of needs – one of their specialities was carpet beating. In a large advertisement headed 'Carpet Beating Season 1920', the public was advised that 'all carpets should be taken up and beaten at least once a year, in order that the accumulation of dust may be removed from the floor boards'. Hanningtons would collect the carpets and take them to a field in Hove, north of the Old Shoreham Road where the carpet beating took place, and then return them. Prices depended on carpet types: Kidderminster or Dutch 2d per square yard; velvet pile 4d per square yard; heavy pile or Oriental 6d per square yard.

G. and C. Denyer, undertakers at 24 Richmond Buildings, Brighton, in around 1898. The photograph shows George Denyer, his son Charlie and his daughter Ellen. Prices on the windows are Children's Single Horse Funeral £1 1s 0d; Children's Pair Horse Funeral £2 2s 0d; Adult Single Horse Funeral £3 0s 0d; Adult Pair Horse Funeral £5 5s 0d.

H.J. Trussell's builder and decorator's business at 11 Market Street, Brighton in around 1901. Mr Trussell established the shop in 1882 and in this photograph Mrs Trussell stands in the doorway. The Trussells had a family of five sons and one daughter. In 1923 Henry Trussell took over as a plumber and by 1924 Mrs E. Trussell was letting apartments on the premises. She continued to live in Market Street until 1941, her bedroom being at the top of the house. The air raid warden frequently had to warn her that the window was not properly blacked out .

C.W. Turner's shop at 26 Southover Street on the corner of Lincoln Street, Brighton in around 1905. Note that he has had 'Cash Grocer' painted above his doorway – a polite way of saying that no credit was allowed here. Butter is on sale for a shilling and tea cost 1s 4d or 1s 6d.

S. Banfield's shop at 56 Ship Street, Brighton in around 1910. It must be something of a local record that there was a Banfield's shop in Ship Street from 1884 until 1970. The business was founded by George Banfield who was a scale maker and gas fitter. The business expanded into shopfitting and, in the later days, into kitchen fitting.

Needham and Sons in around 1905. It occupied a prime position in more ways than one. By 1910 the firm thought nothing of taking a full page advertisement in the *Brighton Herald* at the top of which the Brighton coat of arms lent a certain official air. The store was established in 1848. By 1910 you could buy such items as corsets, feather boas, sunshades, wedding trousseaus, clerical clothing and clothing suitable to wear in motor cars.

The office of the Southern Publishing Company in North Street, Brighton in around 1916. The young ladies were part of the army of young women who took over many jobs when the men were called up. The company published the *Morning Argus* (until 1926), the *Sussex Daily News* (until 1956), the *Southern Weekly News* (until 1965), and of course the *Evening Argus*.

Daniel Shaw, Butterman and Cheesemonger, outside his shop on the corner of George Street, Hove in around 1870. The shop's official address at that time was 11/12 Church Street, Cliftonville. Daniel kept careful records of his trading in his daybook, entered in his neat copperplate writing. The beautiful brass scales and large scoop which he used are still preserved by his descendants. The business was established in 1862.

This photograph was taken in around 1936 and shows how the shop in the previous photograph had expanded into Shaw's Stores. Alfred Shaw had purchased the premises from the Gallard Estate and expanded northwards in the 1920s by taking over a greengrocers and an umbrella and hairdressing shop. In 1934 a new style of shop window was installed, the first in the area. It was known as invisible glass because it was curved in such a way that a customer looking in would not be able to notice there was any glass there. Shaw's Stores closed in 1964.

George Flowers, saddler and harness maker, outside his shop at 64 George Street, Hove in around 1894. His father, also George Flowers, had been killed on 25 October 1854 at Balaclava; he was in the front line of the 17th Lancers at the Charge of the Light Brigade. His wife was with him in the Crimea and after his death she returned to England where her son was born. He was educated at the Star and Garter Home, Richmond.

J. Goldsmith's greengrocer's shop on the corner of Blatchington Road and George Street in around 1921. Mr Goldsmith stands in the doorway behind the boy with a long overall. He married Lily Flowers, daughter of George Flowers, harness maker. Lily stands on the right with her brother Harry Flowers next to her. He had recently returned from war service in Mesopotamia and was employed temporarily by his brother-in-law.

A delightful group of children photographed in George Street in around 1910. On the right the festoons of shoes belong to Freeman, Hardy and Willis, and, standing against the window, complete with smart suit and watch chain, is Harry Flowers who worked in the shop. He was the son of George Flowers, harness maker.

Thomas Walter Wiles' shop at 33 George Street, Hove in around 1910. He established a stationers and toy shop there in 1905 and stayed for twenty-two years. For local historians his claim to fame was as a prolific photographer of local events which he produced as postcards. This shop had a studio and dark-room at the back. It was very much a family enterprise as he was assisted by his daughter Mary and brother George.

William Taylor's shop at 78 Goldstone Villas, Hove in around 1904. The family had moved from the Isle of Wight in 1902 as they thought an expanding town like Hove would provide good business opportunities. William Taylor stands in the doorway and his young son Charles Hugh Taylor (then about eight years old) holds the horse's head. His sister Vera is peeping out from the greenery above the row of poultry. The son inherited the business in 1925.

G.W. Priestley's butcher's shop at 8 Blatchington Road, Hove in around 1900. The large notice in the doorway reads 'Meat of the Finest Quality only sold at this Establishment'.

J. Nelson and Sons' butcher's shop in George Street, Hove in around 1905. The shop was situated at the north end where it lasted for about six years. Competition was stiff in 1907 as there were five other butchers in the same street, plus the Coe brothers who specialized in game as well as selling fresh fish. Nelson's did, however, thrive elsewhere and by 1914 they ran eight butcher's shops in Brighton besides one in Westbourne Street, Hove.

Frank Hart's butcher's shop at 88 Trafalgar Road, Portslade in around 1926. Left to right: old Mr Hart, George Ellis, Reuben Hart and Leslie Garrard. When George Ellis started work in the shop at the age of fifteen in 1924 he earned 10*s* a week and he had to purchase the overalls and striped apron himself. By 1935 George was earning £2 a week and Mr Hart employed six men and a boy.

F.W. and C.A. Hart's radio shop at 79 Trafalgar Road, Portslade in around 1938. The business was established in 1937 and Frank Hart's brother Reuben ran the butcher's shop opposite. Frank Hart was a wireless dealer and many people can remember taking their heavy transformers to be recharged at his shop every three weeks or so. Next door was Frederick Webb's shop; he was a bootmaker and repairer.

A view of Shirley Street, Hove on 15 June 1910. A brass band and a large banner head a crocodile of people going on the Clarendon Mission Outing. The shops on the right are Humphrey's Boot Stores; the Misses E. and K. Pitt, drapers and confectioners; Edward J. Chappell, dealer in all kinds of fish; and George Smith, butcher.

Mr and Mrs J. Charman outside their sweet and tobacconist's shop at Wellington Road, Portslade in 1929. Their daugher Mary stands in front.

Ken Lane's bookshop at 52 Blatchington Road, on the corner of Belfast Street, Hove in March 1985. Shortly after this photograph was taken the shops were knocked down and the site redeveloped. Ken Lane used to be manager of Combridges Antiquarian Bookshop at 70 Church Road which had a huge stock of books relating to Sussex. Ken ran his Blatchington Road bookshop from 1960 until 1985 and his particular interest was books about the circus.

A. Pierce and Son's ironmonger's shop at 24–5 Station Road, Portslade in 1928. In the doorway stands Bert Pierce and Maud Osborn (later to be Mrs Pierce). The business was founded by Bert Pierce's father in 1916 at No. 25 and Bert himself started work there at the age of thirteen. He should have been at school but preferred to be in the shop.

The Clifton Arms, 25 Clifton Terrace, Brighton in around 1905. The pub seemed to change its proprietors fairly often. In 1905 the proprietor was E.W. Swales; from 1907 until 1911 it was G.T. Terry; in 1912 it was Mrs R. Betts; from 1913 until 1914 it was Harry Hall and in 1915 it was Mrs B. Hall.

William Lynn and his wife and daughter outside the Ship Inn, Hove Street in around 1912. Lynn was proprietor from 1911 until 1920. The Ship was a historic place with smuggling associations. The landlord also used to serve hot dinners to the spectators of the bull baiting which took place opposite. The council wanted to straighten out the old street and so the Ship Inn was demolished in 1915 and the Ship Hotel was built further back from the road.

The Southern Cross pub on the corner of Trafalgar Road and the Old Shoreham Road, Portslade in around 1901. The man is most probably George Ashman, the proprietor from around 1896 until the 1920s. In this photograph the pub is owned by Chapman and Co. but by 1904 it had been taken over by Rock Brewery. The pub survived until the 1970s when it was demolished for road widening.

The Windmill Inn, Portslade with decorations and floodlighting for King George V's Silver Jubilee in May 1935. The landlord at the time was G.W. Hazelgrove. The pub was situated near to where the old Copperas Gap windmill stood before it was demolished in around 1872.

The Gardener's Arms, Portslade in the 1940s. The landlord Cecil E. Grainger stands second left from the man with the accordion. The Graingers were associated with the pub for about thirty years.

SECTION ELEVEN

Park and Gardens

The entrance to Preston Park by the South Gates in 1906. Preston Park was the first and largest of Brighton's parks and civic pride is displayed in the magnificent gates, piers and railings, not to mention the ornamental lamps. The park, originally over 60 acres of meadow land, was purchased by Brighton in 1883. A bookmaker called William Davies had bequeathed a large sum to the town out of which the £50,000 purchase money was taken.

Queen's Park, Brighton in around 1920. The magnificent red brick and terracotta fountain was erected in 1893. It is a monument to the fact that the park was purchased by the Race Stand Trustees for £9,504, and presented to the town in 1891. The Race Stand Trustees then added a further sum to pay for the cost of laying out the grounds.

Queen's Park, Brighton in 1912. This delightful postcard depicts children enjoying themselves in the open air. The fountain is on the left and there is a little stream leading to the lake on the right.

The lake, Queen's Park in around 1918. It is difficult to imagine that this graceful lake with its swans was once a huge roller skating rink in the late nineteenth century.

Blaker's Park, Brighton in around 1920. Compared to Preston Park, Blaker's Park is tiny, being just over 4 acres. Brighton has been fortunate in its benefactors as this park too was a donation to the town. It was given by John George Blaker who also paid £1,000 for the steel and cast iron clock tower to be erected (on the left of the photograph). It stands 50 feet high and he inaugurated it himself in 1896 when he was mayor.

Hollingbury Park in around 1910. This well-wooded section was planted early in the nineteenth century but many trees were lost in 1987. Hollingbury Golf Course covers much of the park area.

The entrance gates to Stanmer Park in around 1905. Three factors have combined to alter Stanmer Park drastically: the building of the University of Sussex, the storm in 1987, and the construction of the Brighton bypass. The following passage was published in 1885. The house 'stands about a mile from the lodges in the road from Lewes to Brighton, nearly in the centre of the fine park, whose undulating surface is varied by thick masses of rich foliage forming a striking contrast to the open Downs by which it is surrounded'.

Victoria Gardens in 1910. The gardens were opened for public use on Queen Victoria's Diamond Jubilee in 1897 but the railings date from the time when they were private gardens. They can still be seen on the left.

Victoria Gardens, c. 1928. The gardens were remodelled in around 1922 and have become less secluded. The tall railings and the shrubbery have gone, the pavement has been broadened, and the grass is divided off by dwarf fencing. Note the large mature tree on the right.

Royal Pavilion eastern lawns in 1927. The graceful balustrade was erected in the early 1920s and the pool was created at the same time. Part of the balustrade was smashed in 1987 when a tree crashed on to it in the October storm, but it has been carefully restored.

Royal Pavilion western lawns in 1905. Except for the Pavilion in the background, this view is virtually unrecognizable today. Many of the trees have gone, as have the formal flower beds and the bandstand with its attendant seating. In the 1980s the grounds were redesigned back to the original plan.

St Ann's Well Gardens, Hove in around 1910. The band is playing in a temporary bandstand but in 1912 Hove Council purchased a permanent structure. The 4th (Royal Irish) Dragoon Guards were frequent summer visitors to Hove, playing every year from 1909 until 1913. In 1910 it cost £651 18s 0d to hire the Guards for a season and this was paid for by the special ½d rate and the sale of programmes. The band committee even made a small profit.

An exceedingly bleak view of Hove Park in around 1912. Not everybody thought a new park was a good idea. Councillor Bruce Morison protested that it was 'useless expenditure and the money would be better laid out on artisans' dwellings'. Yet it was he, in his capacity as mayor, who formally opened it three years later in 1906. The land had been part of Goldstone Farm and in 1901 it had produced broccoli, cauliflower, potatoes, cabbage, Brussels sprouts and parsley, with asparagus being the main crop.

Victoria Recreation Ground, Portslade in around 1910. The site was a former brickfield and there were still brickfields to the east of it when the purchase was made. The site cost £2,350 and the park was opened in 1902 with 1,300 children present. Portslade Band was permitted to play sacred music on Sundays after 5 p.m. in the summer, but no collection was allowed.

Easthill Park, Portslade in around 1955. Easthill House on the left was once one of the grand houses of Portslade. It was lived in by the Blaker family who farmed over 500 acres. The house, together with the surrounding 6 acres, was purchased by Portslade Urban District Council in 1947. Note the late lamented palm tree flourishing in the foreground.

Events

The visit of Princess Mary on 23 November 1921. Princess Mary certainly had a full schedule: she inspected the Girl Guides at the Royal Pavilion, opened the new nurses' home at the Royal Sussex County Hospital and, at the Dome, accepted purses on behalf of the Girls' Friendly Society. She also lunched with the Earl and Countess of Chichester at Stanmer Park and took tea with the mayor and mayoress at the Royal Pavilion. However, thousands of spectators were disappointed when she was driven past in a 'closed and fleeting motor car'. The *Brighton Gazette* concluded that somebody had blundered badly. The princess wore a mole grey costume, a grey fox fur and she carried a skunk muff. Next morning the newspapers were full of the official announcement of her betrothal to Viscount Lascelles, son and heir of the Earl of Harewood.

The visit of the Prince of Wales to Brighton on 1 February 1921. The prince unveiled the Chattri at Patcham – a memorial in white marble on the place where the Hindu and Sikh soldiers who had died at Brighton were cremated. The photograph shows the prince accompanied by the mayor Alderman Bertram Southall. In the background can be seen the Phoenix Assurance Co. at 9 North Street Quadrant and next door is A.J. Day's dental surgery offering 'painless extractions'.

The Prince of Wales's visit, 1 February 1921. The photograph was taken during the second part of the prince's visit. After the formal unveiling of the Chattri and the loyal address of welcome at the Dome, the prince changed into mufti and visited workshops for the disabled. He opened the new Lord Robert's Memorial Workshops and visited the Bernard Oppenheimer Diamond Works for disabled men.

The visit of the Duke and Duchess of York to Brighton, 17 October 1924. In the morning the royal couple visited Ronuk's Factory at Portslade, followed by lunch at Hove Town Hall after which they opened a hobbies and handicraft exhibition. In the afternoon the duke and duchess inspected a huge crowd of local youth organizations in the grounds of the Royal Pavilion. The duchess wore a coat and skirt of rust red velour and a black cloche hat adorned with a diamond arrow and rust ostrich feathers.

Red Cross cadets in the grounds of the Royal Pavilion. It seems likely that this photograph was taken on the day the Duke and Duchess of York visited Brighton, 17 October 1924. In the background at 10 Pavilion Parade is a boarding house called Belmont. This must have been confusing for the postmen because there were fifteen houses so named in the Brighton and Hove area.

The visit of the Duke and Duchess of York to Brighton, 30 May 1928. The duchess wears a dress of beige crêpe and a long coat of georgette trimmed with fox fur. Her closely-fitting hat is adorned with a diamond brooch and an osprey plume. The duke and duchess are seen here leaving the Royal Alexandra Hospital for Children after opening a new wing, constructed at a cost of £12,000.

The duke and duchess receive gifts, 30 May 1928. The royal couple are standing outside the Royal Alexandra Hospital for Children and they have just been presented with some dolls (one dressed as a nurse) for two year old Princess Elizabeth.

Moreland's Annual Outing, 15 June 1907. The staff of Richard Moreland and Sons, engineers, are pictured above at what appears to be an exclusively male jamboree. The decorated hall in West Street, Brighton had formerly been a roller skating rink. Four years after this photograph was taken the hall was converted into a cinema, but in 1919 it became Sherry's Dance Hall.

French visitors, 15 August 1907. When the French bands arrived at Brighton they were warmly welcomed in French by the Mayor, Councillor Henry Gervis. The Municipal Band of Calais, numbering seventy-five performers, gave a concert on the eastern lawns. The William Tell overture and Donjon's Rondo for Flute, the solo finely played by M.J. Leuliette, were heartily applauded.

The opening of Hove Public Library by the Countess of Jersey, 8 July 1908. The countess is accompanied by her daughter Lady Margaret Rice and the Mayor of Hove, Alderman A.B.S. Fraser. The library was designed by W.A. Jones and P. Robinson of Leeds and Andrew Carnegie donated £10,000 towards the building costs.

Lewes Road congregational church outing, 5 July 1909. July was an extremely busy time on the railways with all sorts of clubs, societies and industrial concerns going on their annual outings. It was probably the reason why this group chose to travel on a Monday.

Laying the foundation stone of the extension of St Philip's church, Hove, 12 February 1910. The Rector of Aldrington, the Revd E.J. Morgan, was keen to see St Philip's as a separate parish but the ecclesiastical commissioners stipulated that parish churches must be able to accommodate 500 people – hence the extension. A delightful touch in this photograph of solemn men is the line of washing flapping above the Bishop of Lewes' head.

Coronation Day, 22 June 1911. The scene is Victoria Park, Portslade shortly after the grand procession had arrived. The men belonged to various Portslade friendly societies such as the Abinger Lodge of Buffaloes, the Ancient Order of Foresters and the Sons of Temperance Benefit Society. The procession had been accompanied by the Portslade town band and the combined fife and drum bands of St Nicolas Band of Hope and the Baptist Sunday school. An incredible 1,800 coronation mugs were presented to local children.

Sunday school outing, Portslade, 1914. The Portslade Amalgamated Sunday Schools march up Station Road, past the Railway Inn, to the station for their trip to Hassocks. Albert and Olive Pierce are on the left – he is wearing a straw boater and she wears a dark hat with feather trimmings.

Brighton answers Kitchener 1914. Within a few days of becoming Secretary of State for War, Earl Kitchener launched his famous proclamation on 11 August 1914 'Your King and Country Needs You. A Call to Arms'. The first poster carried only the lettering; later ones carried Kitchener's portrait and pointing finger and the slogan was shortened. In less than two weeks 100,000 men between nineteen and thirty had volunteered.

Hove Allotment Holders' Association Annual Show, 1919. A fine view of the Great Hall at Hove Town Hall. Note the organ in the background, constructed by the famous organ builder Henry Willis which was sold seven years before the town hall was gutted by fire.

Hove Horticultural and Allotment Holders' Association 7th Annual Show. Note how the association acquired an extra 'H' as it moved up market. It had come a long way since the first show was held at the Ralli Hall in 1917 – the result of a move to grow fresh vegetables and beat wartime shortages. One of the 1917 postcards showed a trestle table groaning under the weight of several large marrows with the glorious caption 'Fruits of Labour and Heavenly Blessings on the Council Allotments'.

The Committee of the Hove Horticultural and Allotment Holders' Association in 1923.
At the back, left to right: -?-, -?-, Mr Butterworth, Mr Dowman, Mr Heavens and Mr
Jenkins. In the second row the man on the far left with the high wing collar is Mr
Brooks who had an ironmonger's shop in Blatchington Road; Mr Slater is third from
the right and Mrs Heavens is on the far right. The mayor and mayoress are seated in the
front – the mayor was often president of the association.

One of the floats which took part in the Brighton carnival of 1922. The framed picture
on the front shows four teddy bears and there is a teddy bear sitting on the lion's head
on the left above a notice saying 'Beware of the Dog'.

Brighton carnival, 1923. The two Spanish looking gentlemen are carrying an advertisement attached to the horse's blanket which says 'Royal Pavilion Grounds. A Bull Fight To-night'. One of the men is Fred Miller, later a Hove alderman, who had a shop in George Street and subsequently at Blatchington Road where Sainsbury's was until recently.

Brighton carnival, 1923. This is the bull fight advertised in the previous photograph. The bull is in the tradition of a pantomime horse, with two men inside the costume while the three extraordinary looking horses in the ring are operated by one man and resemble a glorified hobby horse.

A garden party on the vicarage lawn at St Nicolas's, Portslade. The old vicarage, a huge barn of a place, was demolished in the 1960s after a new vicarage had been built further to the east. The old lady in the foreground has a somewhat ferocious expression while on the right the young family have placed the child's teddy bear on a chair of its own looking at the camera.

Silver Wedding celebrations, 1938. The venue is Rothbury Hall in Franklin Road, Portslade, and the happy couple are Charles Ernest and Charlotte Mary Forrest. There is an elaborate wedding cake at the top table from which garlands are looped to the three wings of the other tables.

A wartime wedding reception on 14 April 1942. The guests look happy but a little cramped as they are all squashed into a room at 14 Abinger Road, Portslade. Reg Forrest, the bridegroom, can be seen in the background wearing his RAF uniform with his bride Gwen. The man in profile in the left foreground is Tom Puttock, chief engineer at the Mile Oak Waterworks.

The funeral of William Alled, a Crimean veteran, at Rottingdean, 31 March 1909. He enlisted in the Army in 1853 and served for twenty-two years, first in the 101st Foot Regiment and afterwards with the 84th. He served all through the Crimean War and the Indian Mutiny. At his funeral his coffin was borne by six Guardsmen, and the band of the 4th (Royal Irish) Dragoon Guards played under the direction of Bandmaster H. Dudley.

The Vicar of Hove's funeral, 6 April 1909. When the Revd Prebendary Thomas Peacey died on 1 April it was almost thirty years to the day since he had been appointed vicar of Hove. He set about restoring St Andrew's old church, building St Barnabas's church and vicarage, rebuilding the National Schools in George Street and erecting Hove vicarage. His chief claim to fame, however, was the building of the magnificent All Saints church. He must have been a man of some energy because he also had a large family of seven daughters and three sons.

The Vicar of Hove's funeral, 6 April 1909. The high regard in which Canon Peacey was held can be gauged from the fact that some forty clergymen were present, as well as the Bishop of Chichester and the mayors of Brighton and Hove. This photograph is particularly interesting because of the inadvertent portrait of the grave-digger in the left foreground. Note the tough working trousers secured below the knee as was the custom.

An open-air service for the late King Edward VII, 20 May 1910. This was necessary because All Saints was packed to capacity and the Bishop of Lewes had just finished conducting a service there before he took the alfresco one. Only three months previously the king had attended morning service at All Saints and the Bishop of Lewes preached the sermon.

Hove's floral tribute to the late King Edward VII was in the form of the Hove coat of arms although the leg-irons of St Leonard appear to have become a little scrambled. Hove's feeling of loss at the king's death was also tinged with regret that he had not had time to build himself a residence in the town. There had been high hopes that he might, having paid frequent visits to the Sassoons and found the air beneficial.

Lilian Hibberd's funeral, 30 September 1910. Lilian, a young lady of twenty-seven, lived at 13 Portland Road, Hove. She was riding her bicycle down Tisbury Road and in crossing Church Road to go to Third Avenue, she collided with a motor bus. Newspaper accounts were more graphic: 'the wheel of the vehicle passed over her head, completely smashing the skull, and death was, of course, practically instantaneous'. A large crowd watched the coffin being carried into Holy Trinity church. There was also a floral tribute from the employees of the Brighton and Hove General Omnibus Co.

James Tree's funeral at Hove, 3 June 1911. James Tree had spent all his life at Hove and was the verger at St Andrew's church for about thirty years. The view looks south to St Aubyns. Note the absence of the lich-gate which was not erected until the 1950s. In the background, the conservatory roof belonged to William Balchin and Sons, florists, seedsmen and nurserymen.

Part of the 1953 Hove College school photograph. The teaching staff are from left to right: Mrs Glastonbury, Mr Randell, Dr M.A. Gubert, Mrs Y. Kenworthy, Mr M. Sellers, Mr J. Dickson, Mr R.L.C. Jackson, Mrs R.R. Jackson, Mr F. Brown, Mr C.F. Beauclerk and Mr Collenette. The tall boy standing behind Mr Jackson is Andrew Cregeen, now proprietor and manager of the Hovedene Hotel. In the front row the little boy fourth from the right is David Barling, later to be Mayor of Hove 1983–4.

A classroom at Hove College in 1913. The boys are being taught by the headmaster, Mr E.C. Jackson. The school was founded in 1796 and continued until 1980. The school motto was *Rege Recte* (steer straight) and the colours were claret and grey.

GIRTON HOUSE,
2, 3, and 4, WALSINGHAM MANSIONS,
BRIGHTON.

VIEW FROM GIRTON HOUSE.

Girton House, Walsingham Mansions, Hove *c.* 1905. This was a school for girls started by Mrs Beney-Willis in 1904; it lasted until 1934. On Sundays the girls wore cream pleated skirts with a cream jacket and hat encircled with the school ribbon. They attended St Philip's church where they were supposed to keep their eyes on their hymn books and not look at the Hove College boys who also attended the church.

Brighton Grammar School decorated for the coronation of George V, 22 June 1911. The banner around the top of the building reads 'King of the United Kingdom of Great Britain and Ireland and of all the British Dominions beyond the Seas'. The building in Buckingham Road, designed by a Mr Nunn, was home to the school from 1868 until 1913. Subsequently it became the Sussex Maternity Hospital.

The Brighton, Hove and Sussex Grammar School in 1914. This magnificent building was erected at a cost of £25,000 to the designs of S.B. Russell. It was ready for occupation by 1913 but the boys from Buckingham Road had barely time to settle in before the whole school was commandeered by the authorities. It served as a military hospital from 1914 until 1919.

Wistons School, Brighton in around 1930. The school was proud of its hard court, laid in 1929. It certainly made a change from running round Dyke Park which was all the exercise on offer before. The girls are dressed in their uniform of chocolate brown gym slips with a purple sash. The school tie had purple and white stripes. In the background can be seen the turret of the grammar school.

Wistons School, Brighton in around 1930 showing the landing and office. Note the old fashioned telephone on the window sill of the office. Wistons was a private girls' school founded in 1915. It spent its early years in a large house on the corner of the Old Shoreham Road before moving to these premises in 1920 when the number of pupils had risen to ninety.

Wistons School, Brighton in around 1930. This view is rather grandly entitled 'The Aquaria'. No doubt it was meant to impress the parents of prospective pupils because science lessons of any description were still quite unusual in private girls' schools of the time. The school motto was 'Strive and Thrive' and the crest was the winged horse Pegasus.

St Mary's Hall, Brighton in around 1915. At the time this photograph was taken the school was still exclusively for the daughters of clergymen. The school was opened in 1836 and the architect was George Basevi, the same man who was also responsible for the rebuilding of St Andrew's old church, Hove at about the same time. The girls are engaged in gardening, an occupation for ladies popularized by Viscountess Wolseley, who founded the Glynde College of Gardening.

St Nicolas's Girls' School, Portslade in around 1907. Mrs Sayers supervises her girls as they do some gentle exercise with Indian clubs. The girls' school had been a separate department since 1883. Their education was biased towards the domestic sphere with emphasis on sewing, knitting, mending and how to do the washing, but arithmetic, penmanship and religious education were important too, and the inspector had no fault to find with their grammar.

The teachers of St Nicolas's Girls' School in around 1911. Left to right, back row: -?-, Miss Elsie Sayers, Miss Winifred Terry; front row: Mrs Austin, Mrs Mary Florence Sayers, Mrs Bringloe and Miss Lodge. When the headmistress, Mrs Sayers, celebrated twenty-five years of service in 1912 she received a silver plated tea and coffee service.

SECTION FOURTEEN

Military Presence

Brighton Camp, Hollingbury Park in around 1906. Presumably one of the first duties of a volunteer on his arrival in camp was to stuff his palliasse with straw – hardly the most comfortable of mattresses but preferable to the hard ground. There were compensations, however, such as free entrance to the West Pier or Palace Pier for soldiers in uniform. In August 1906 the *Brighton Gazette* reported that the variety of uniforms on the seafront was endless.

The East Surrey Brigade at Hollingbury Park in August 1904. For two years in succession the East Surrey Brigade camped here. The brigade consisted of the 1st Surrey Rifles, 2nd Wimbledon, 3rd Kingston and 4th Clapham Battalions together with the 1st Cadet Battalion Royal West Surrey and the East Surrey Rifle Volunteers. Altogether it was a sizeable camp and the man in charge was Colonel Frodsham. Thousands of people visited the camp daily to watch the drilling, their travel facilitated by the Beaconsfield and Ditchling Road trams.

The East Surrey Brigade, Royal Army Medical Corps Volunteers in around 1906. An army needs its ambulance corps but imagine the jolting an injured soldier would receive, rattling around in one of these conveyances.

Church parade of the 20th Hussars in around 1905. The men attended St Martin's, popularly known as the soldiers' church because of its proximity to the barracks and the number of church parades held there. Appropriately enough, St Martin was a soldier saint. In 1905 there was a polo match in Preston Park between the 2nd Lieutenants' team of the 20th Hussars and the Sussex Imperial Yeomanry. In the summer of 1906 the band of the 20th Hussars was a great success with their concerts on the Hove Lawns.

The Royal Engineers at camp in Portslade in 1914. The camp was established in the playing fields belonging to Windlesham House School and the boys helped to erect the tents. Later in the war a military cookery instruction camp was sited here with some thirty-eight huts.

Australian cadets entering Holy Trinity church, Hove in August 1911. There were 120 of these Australian cadets at Hove, junior and senior members of the South Wales Cadet Corps. They were over here to take part in the coronation festivities in London but had later come to Hove for a change of air. They were billeted at the Holland Road Council Schools. But it was obviously no rest cure as they still had to get up at 5.30 a.m. and parade for bathing at 6 a.m.

Portslade Home Guard outside the Ronuk Hall in 1943. Left to right, front row: Sid Hibbard, Stan Gibbs, Bill Maynard. Second row: Ted Perry, Matt Coomber, Lieut. Smith, Lieut. Richards, Sergeant Todd and Cpl. Charlie Clarke. Back row: Bob Partner, Dixie Dean, Len Souter, Arthur Harrison and Len Searle. The Ronuk Hall became a British restaurant during the war.

SECTION FIFTEEN

Vanishing Countryside

A harvest field at West Blatchington in around 1920. The buildings belong to Toad's Hole Farm – a curious name which seems to date back only to the last century; it appears on the 1879 Ordnance Survey map. The diagonal line of bushes marks the old track over the Downs, now the site of King George VI Avenue.

The valley of Mile Oak, Portslade as it was in 1935 looking west to the Industrial School on the horizon. The sheep on Mr Broomfield's farm are enclosed in pens made of hurdles traditionally constructed from woven hazel. The gap in the centre of each panel was put there on purpose to make carrying them easier.

Paddocks Tea Garden, Portslade in around 1910. The area was a racing stables in 1871 and by the 1890s the Paddocks was said to be one of the best stables ever visited by a reporter from the *Racing Illustrated*. Famous names associated with the stables were T.J. Widger and Joe Widger, the latter winning the 1895 Grand National on *Wild Man from Borneo*. The jockey was no lightweight as he weighed in at 10 stones 11 pounds. In later years the Paddocks became a tea garden.

The green valley of Mile Oak, Portslade in around 1946. The view looks towards Southwick Hill and on the left there are a few houses in Mile Oak Road. In the middle ground is the newly built senior girls' school. The procession is making its way along a track, later to become Chalky Road, towards the church of the Good Shepherd (popularly called the tin hut) which was dedicated in 1936.

Mile Oak, Portslade in 1958. Contrast this view with the previous one as this time the photographer was facing east. The senior girls' school is no longer out on its own – the bungalows in the foreground on the east side of Valley Road were built in around 1955.

A view of Warren Farm School in 1909. The school was built at Woodingdean in 1858 to accommodate destitute children whose parents were in the workhouse. In 1914 children as young as three were being sent there. The girls were trained for domestic work and the boys learned trades such as bootmaking and gardening. The need for fresh water on this isolated site led to the digging of a well which took from 1858 to 1862. With a depth of 1,285 ft it is the deepest hand-dug well in the world. It was rediscovered in 1994.

A building site on the corner of Portland Avenue and New Church Road in 1908. Albert Pierce is the figure on the right with a straw hat and cane and his brother George leans against the wall wearing braces and a flat cap. Aldrington was an area of flat land perfect for housing development. In the early years of the last century nobody lived there – there were still only 144 residents in 1881.

SECTION SIXTEEN

Groups

Brighton Corporation Band in 1907. In June 1907 Brighton councillors approved the hiring of Herr Franz Meisel and his Imperial Austrian Band to undertake engagements as the corporation band. It was a controversial decision not least because, out of twenty-seven members, only eleven were Englishmen. Local musicians were furious. The example of Hove was quoted – Hove had hired a military band, every man of whom was a Brightonian. Meisel's band was composed of six 1st violins, two 2nd violins, two cellos, two double bass, one flute, one piccolo, one oboe, two clarinets, one bassoon, two horns, two cornets, one trombone, one euphonium, drums and cymbals.

The Salvation Army Band outside the Brighton Congress Hall in around 1908. The young drummer reclining on the left is Arthur Pumphrey who served in France during the latter part of the First World War together with several other band members who formed a special ambulance unit. The bandmaster is probably a Mr Day who, in 1913, was said to have been bandmaster of the Brighton No. 1 Corps for sixteen years. His wife died in 1913 aged 47 and hymns sung at her graveside included 'When the Roll is called up Yonder' and 'Nearer my God to Thee'.

Brighton Divisional Staff in 1925. These Salvation Army officers are as follows. Left to right, front row: Mrs Lieut.-Col. Starling, Lieut.-Col. Starling (Divisional Commander), Major Smith (Divisional Youth Secretary) and Mrs Major Smith. Back row: Captain Jeanie Roberts (Divisional Secretary), -?-, and Miss Elsie Smith.

Ellison's All Lady Concert Party, Brighton, 1918. When men were needed for the show, some of the girls had to dress the part.

By 1919 the group's title had changed to Ellison's Entertainers, probably because it now contained some young men back from the war. The huge crowd they attracted included everyone from grandpa in the front row to children perched uncomfortably on the wall at the back.

The cast of *Merrie England*, performed by the Brighton and Hove Operatic Society at the Theatre Royal, Brighton, May 1907. The cast included Reginald Hobson (Earl of Essex), Florence Donovan (Bessie Throckmorton), Wallis Long (Sir Walter Raleigh) and Ella Leggatt (Queen Elizabeth). The *Brighton Gazette* predicted that Hobson's rendering of 'Yeoman of England' would bring the house down. It did.

British Women's Garden Party, 1911. You could almost call this an essay on hats. Note how the younger women are wearing large picture hats with plenty of trimmings while the older women wear small close-to-the-head hats in a style popular when they were young.

Band of Hope Demonstration, 1913. The Band of Hope was a temperance organization which aimed to protect children and young people from the demon drink. In 1913 there were 176 Band of Hope societies in Sussex with a juvenile membership of 14,245 plus 950 adult workers, making a grand total of 15,195.

St Andrew's Boys' Club, Portslade in around 1913, run by Mr Bear who stands on the far left wearing a straw boater. In the third row Mrs Drew is seated third from the left wearing a large hat and next to her on the left is her daughter whose future husband Doug Mepham stands behind her.

The caption for this postcard reads 'Entertaining our Brave Wounded Soldiers, 1915'. The fashionable ladies vied with each other to entertain the wounded soldiers. During the summer there was a tea party almost every week. One of the most stalwart workers was Mrs Pollak who practically made a career of ferrying the soldiers to and from parties, as well as waiting at Brighton station to greet them on arrival. She was presented to the Prince of Wales in 1921.

The Co-operative Women's Guild (Portslade Branch) on an outing to the Northampton Shoe Factory in about 1932. The Brighton Co-operative Society was founded in 1887 and by 1921 it had 10,000 members. As well as the famous dividend, the society also promoted educational and social functions. In the photograph Mrs Todd is in the front row, second from left.

SECTION SEVENTEEN
Demolished Churches

The Dials congregational church, Dyke Road, on the corner of Clifton Road, Brighton. This magnificent structure was erected in 1871 to the design of Thomas Simpson. Its Romanesque features and Rhineland-type tower made it a considerable landmark. In 1969 the church was sold for £30,000 and it was demolished in 1972.

Union church, Queen's Square, Brighton in 1906. It was built in the 1850s as a Baptist church and closed in 1904 when the Baptists moved to Gloucester Place. From 1904 until 1948 it was a Free church, and was demolished in 1984.

All Soul's, Eastern Road, Brighton, 1915. This church was built specifically for the poor by the Revd Henry Michell Wagner. It cost just over £3,000, with £1,000 being donated by the Brighton clergy. Small amounts were also given by fishermen and locally based soldiers. The church was designed by Messrs Mews and was consecrated on 4 April 1834. It was demolished in 1968.

Christ Church, Montpelier Road, Brighton in 1905. The church was designed by George Cheeseman and consecrated by the Bishop of Chichester on 26 April 1838. This church too was built under the auspices of the Revd Henry Michell Wagner and as usual all the Wagners contributed to the cost, including his mother and sister. Father Wagner also paid for the stained glass in the east window. The reredos included the Creed on the left and the Lord's Prayer on the right.

Christ Church, Montpelier Road, Brighton in 1905. The stained glass given by Father Wagner can be clearly seen. There are also panels on either side of the altar with the Ten Commandments. Originally there was a large pulpit obscuring the Communion table but the church was remodelled in 1886 by Edmund Scott and the pulpit was moved to the side. The church was badly damaged by fire in 1978 and demolished in 1982.

St James's church, St James's Street, Brighton in 1906. The church was originally used by Dissenters but in 1826 it was consecrated as an Anglican church. It rose to national prominence in the 1860s when the Revd James Purchas was the incumbent. He used incense, candles and vestments at his services which literally caused riots in the streets of Brighton and a crisis in the Diocese of Chichester. The church was demolished in 1950.

Countess of Huntingdon church, North Street, Brighton. This church was built in 1871 to the design of John Wimble in complete contrast to the site's former church which had four massive Ionic columns. The church was closed in 1966. The spire was the first to go, being demolished in 1969, and the rest of the building followed in 1972.

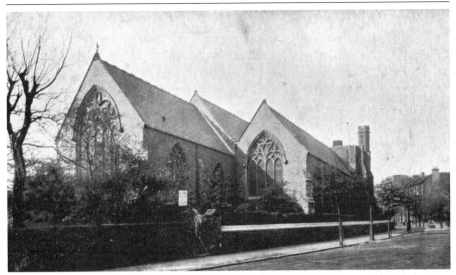

All Saints, Compton Avenue, Brighton in 1904. This was another of the Revd Henry Wagner's churches. It was designed by R.C. Carpenter and erected by George Cheeseman in 1850–2. As can be seen in this photograph the church had a small stumpy tower with an odd little turret jutting up. The church was demolished in 1957.

St Margaret's church, St Margaret's Place, Brighton. The church was almost certainly designed by Charles Augustin Busby. It was in the Greek revival style with an Ionic portico and a cupola in the form of a Tower of the Winds. The church opened in 1824. Most experts agree that it was the most graceful of Brighton's churches but that did not prevent it from being demolished in June 1959.

St Cuthbert's Presbyterian church, Holland Road, Hove. The architect Edmund Proctor designed the church in bold red brick and terracotta and the tower and spire were particularly striking. The church was opened in 1912. One famous minister (from 1919–38) was the Revd Andrew Young, the nature poet, who during his time at Hove published ten volumes of poetry. The church was demolished in 1984.

The Baptist church, North Street, Portslade in around 1905. The foundation stone was laid on 1 October 1891 and the chapel opened the following year. Special weekday services were held for the men who worked at the Gas Works and could not attend on Sundays. At that time the Baptists had the largest Sunday school and Temperance band in the district. In the 1950s the Baptists moved to Portslade Old Village, and the North Street site was sold for £8,300 in 1959. The structure was used as a paper store before eventually being demolished.

Our Lady, Star of the Sea and St Denis Roman Catholic church, Portslade. The church was in July 1912, the money having been provided by Mrs Broderick, a devout widow. It was intended originally that the church should have a flint exterior but the plan was not carried through.

The Lady chapel in the Catholic church, Portslade. The church also boasted frescoes and a baldachin. A tremendous row broke out in the summer of 1992 when it was revealed that the church was to be demolished, and angry parishioners even appealed to the Pope. It was, however, all to no avail, and the church was quickly demolished in July and August 1992.

Acknowledgements

The author would like to thank the following people for kindly loaning their photographs:

The late Miss Muriel Anderson • Mrs G. Banfield • Mr John Broomfield Mrs Browning • Mr John Bryon • the late Mr C. Caperon Miss Ethel Chandler • Mrs J. Eggleton • Mrs F.W. Elliott • Mrs E. Ellis Mrs Field • Mr H.J.G. Flowers • Mr Reg Forrest • Miss M. Frost the late Mr Don Gates • Mr Bob Gill • Mrs L. Hale • Mr Les Hamilton Mrs J. Hayward • Mrs G. Hughes • Mrs R. Jackson • Mr Robert Jeeves of the Picture Postcard Saloon, Queen's Road, Brighton • Mr Terry Jeeves Mr D. Lucas • Mrs Marriot • Mr E. Masters • Mr T. McKendrick-Warden Mr John Melville • Mr A.G.W. Penney • Mr C. Peters • the late Mr Bert Pierce Mr P. Prior • Mr Bill Ring • Miss D. Scrase • Mr Norman Shaw Mrs Audrie Smith • Mr and Mrs Steele • Mr John Tate • Mr D.H. Taylor Mr A.C. Todd • Mrs F. Trussell • Mr R.A. Uridge • Mrs Wakeford Mr and Mrs N. Wheatley.

Thanks are also due to the East Sussex County Library.